FETAL ALCOHOL SYNDROME

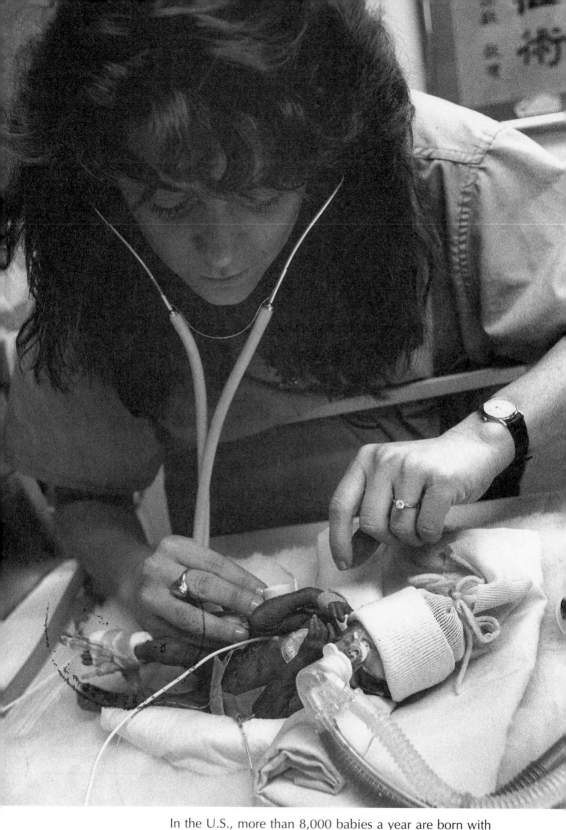

In the U.S., more than 8,000 babies a year are born with fetal alcohol syndrome.

THE DRUG ABUSE PREVENTION LIBRARY

FETAL ALCOHOL SYNDROME

Amy Nevitt

THE ROSEN PUBLISHING GROUP, INC.
NEW YORK

With love and gratitude to the children of Zuni, who have
taught me so much.

Published in 1996 by The Rosen Publishing Group, Inc.
29 East 21st Street, New York, NY 10010

First Edition

Library of Congress Cataloging-in-Publication Data
Nevitt, Amy.
    Fetal alcohol syndrome / Amy Nevitt.
        p.   cm. — (The Drug abuse prevention library)
    Includes bibliographical references and index.
    Summary: Discusses the dangers of consuming
alcohol while pregnant, describes the signs and
symptoms of fetal alcohol syndrome, and suggests
ways to prevent FAS.
    ISBN 0-8239-2061-5
    1. Fetal alcohol syndrome—Juvenile literature.
[1. Fetal alcohol syndrome.   2. Fetus—Effects of
drugs on.]   I. Title.
II. Series.
RG628.3.F45N48   1996
618.3′268—dc20   95-10884
                                                          CIP
                                                           AC

Manufactured in the United States of America

Contents

Introduction

When Mary Ann and her boyfriend, Geoff, heard about the graduation party at Jennie's, they couldn't wait to go. When they got there, Jennie's parents weren't home, but her older sister was. She was collecting money for beer. Mary Ann was a little uncomfortable with the situation, but she decided to stick around. She wanted to prove to Geoff that she could party. Besides, she wanted his friends to like her. She was nervous, so she chugged down the beer Geoff gave her. That made her feel less nervous, so she had another. The music was loud, and everyone was having a good time. Mary Ann ended up having too good a time.

The next day she had a bad headache and felt nauseated. She had a hangover. She

even threw up. She couldn't quite remember
what had happened the night before. Her
mother looked disturbed, but she didn't say
anything; she just pretended everything was
normal. That night Geoff called. He said he
had had a great time and asked her to a
party the next weekend. Mary Ann was
thrilled. She figured she had made a good
impression at Jennie's.

There was a party nearly every weekend
that summer. Mary Ann never noticed that
she stopped getting her period. She did notice
that she was gaining weight, but everyone
said that beer made you fat. She dieted and
tried not to eat too much.

Mary Ann had no idea what she was
going to do with her life. It seemed that a lot
of her classmates were going away to college.
She had no plans. She just partied with
Geoff and his friends all summer.

One morning Mary Ann felt extremely
sick. Finally she went to the health clinic.
The doctor asked a lot of questions, such as
when she had her last period. Mary Ann
couldn't remember. The doctor ran some tests,
then told Mary Ann that she was pregnant.
He asked about her eating habits and
whether she used drugs, smoked cigarettes, or
drank alcohol. He said these things could
hurt the baby. Mary Ann was shocked. She

No one knows exactly how much or how little alcohol
a woman can drink before it affects her unborn baby.

couldn't believe what was happening to her. She thought that she and Geoff had been careful. Then she remembered Jennie's party five months before.

Mary Ann was ashamed. She didn't want to tell the doctor she had been drinking. She didn't want to tell her mother she was pregnant. She was afraid of what would happen when Geoff found out. Mary Ann didn't go back to the doctor. She didn't tell Geoff or her mother that she was pregnant. She decided to pretend that there was nothing different in her life.

One day Mary Ann's mother noticed how big Mary Ann was. She noticed that Mary Ann always wore baggy clothes, but that she hardly ever ate. When she said that she was worried, Mary Ann began to cry. She told her mother everything. Her mother said that she would have to tell Geoff. When she finally did, Geoff said that the baby wasn't his and that he never wanted to see her again. Mary Ann became depressed. The only thing that made her feel better was drinking.

Mary Ann stayed at home. She hadn't gone on to college like her friends. She felt too depressed to find a job. She felt that her mother hated her for getting pregnant. Whenever she could, she went out with her friends and drank.

10 *Near the end of her pregnancy, Mary Ann finally went back to the clinic for her prenatal appointment. She had never told the doctor about her drinking, and she had lied about the fact that she hardly ate anything. She hated the baby inside her.*

The baby was born a month early. He had a small head, his eyes looked strange, and there was something wrong with his lips. His nose was small and flat. The doctors recognized that the baby had been born with fetal alcohol syndrome (FAS). Mary Ann couldn't hide her drinking now.

The doctors said that the baby would have problems, that he would be slow to develop, and that he would need extra care. He would have to come back to the hospital for a few operations. Mary Ann didn't really understand, but she was scared. She felt so alone and unhappy. She felt guilty for what she had done to her baby. She understood now that he would never be normal.

Mary Ann took her baby home and named him Justin. Justin cried all the time. It seemed that he never slept. Even holding him and walking with him didn't help. He was hard to feed, too. He just didn't want to eat.

When he was two weeks old, Justin had to go back to the hospital. He was skinny

and hadn't eaten very much. The doctors *11*
said he had pneumonia. He was in the hospital for two weeks. Mary Ann stayed with
him as much as she could; she even slept at
the hospital.

Finally she realized that she could not
take care of Justin. She could not pay the
hospital bills. Justin needed more operations
and special help. After talking to a social
worker, Mary Ann decided to give Justin up
for adoption.

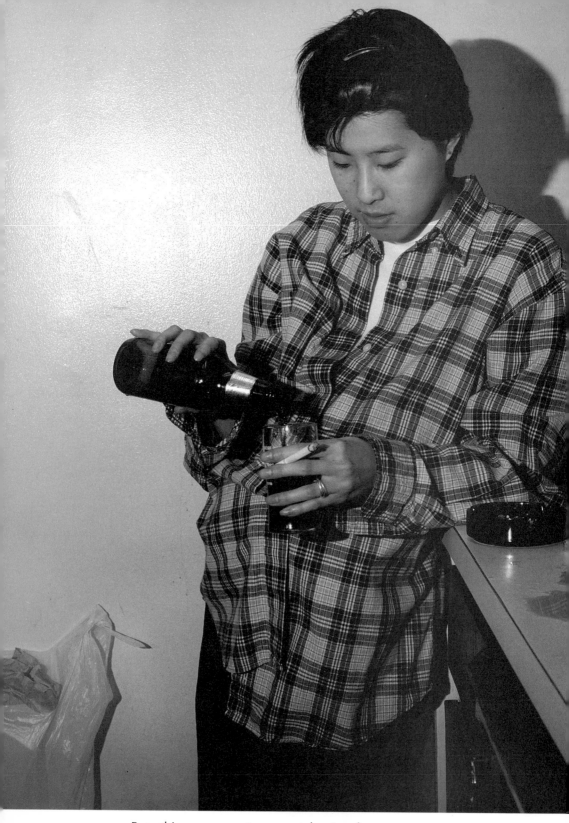

Everything a pregnant woman takes into her body affects the baby inside her.

CHAPTER 1

What Is FAS?

Fetal alcohol syndrome (FAS) is the leading known cause of mental retardation in the West. More than 8,000 babies a year in the U.S. are born with FAS, a birth defect caused by a woman's drinking of alcohol when she is pregnant. It is totally preventable. But because of their mother's alcohol consumption, none of those babies had the chance to be born normal.

About 16 percent of pregnant women drink enough alcohol to be at risk for bearing children with some negative effects. Research shows that the long-term effects of alcohol on fetuses (babies still in the womb) are more powerful than

14 | those of most other drugs, including co-
caine. These effects often fall under the
term "fetal alcohol effect" (FAE). FAE is
not less severe than FAS. FAE means that a
child is born with only some of the symptoms of FAS.

Fetal alcohol syndrome was diagnosed
only about 20 years ago. Until then, people with FAS did not know what was
wrong, why they had so many problems
in life. In 1989 Michael Dorris wrote
about his adopted son, Adam, in the
book *The Broken Cord*. Adam had many
problems growing up. Mr. Dorris spent
several years trying to find out why his
son had such a hard time learning. He
discovered that his son had FAS, a birth
defect he had never heard of before. Mr.
Dorris learned that Adam had been affected by his mother's drinking before he
was even born. He was relieved that there
was a cause for Adam's troubles, although
there was no cure for them. Mr. Dorris
told his story to help other parents and
children learn about the devastating effects of FAS.

People with FAS and FAE can live happy,
productive lives, but a part of them is
affected forever. They will always bear the
effects of their mother's drinking.

CHAPTER 2

Alcohol and Pregnancy

*R*esearch suggests that between one and three babies are born with FAS for every 1,000 live births. And the number of babies born with FAE is much higher.

When a woman is pregnant, everything she eats, drinks, and smokes affects the baby inside her, the fetus. FAS and FAE are caused by drinking alcohol during pregnancy. It is simple to prevent FAS and FAE: Do not drink alcohol during pregnancy.

Alcohol Causes Birth Defects

Alcohol is a *teratogenic* drug. This means that it can cause birth defects. You may have seen this warning on advertisements for and on labels of alcohol: "Government warning: According to the Surgeon

15

The affects of alcohol can be so destructive to unborn babies that a warning to pregnant women is usually found on the labels of alcoholic beverages.

General, women should not drink alcoholic beverages during pregnancy because of the risk of birth defects." The government is warning women that if they drink during pregnancy they can harm their babies.

Alcohol is made by the fermentation of plant sugars and starches with yeast. Beer, "lite" beer, wine, wine coolers, hard liquor (e.g., whiskey, gin, vodka), and liqueurs (e.g., schnapps) all contain alcohol.

Some people think beer or wine is not as strong as hard liquor. That is not true. A glass of wine, a mixed drink, and a

bottle of beer all contain about the same |
amount of alcohol. Some cough and cold medicines and mouthwashes also contain alcohol.

Since no one knows for sure how much alcohol can be consumed without damaging an unborn baby, *it is best to avoid drinking alcohol altogether when pregnant.* A woman who drinks before she knows she is pregnant should stop drinking as soon as she finds out. Ending alcohol consumption at any time during the pregnancy will improve the chances of a healthy baby.

When a Pregnant Woman Drinks

The effects of prenatal (before birth) drinking on a baby can be slight or devastating. A woman planning to get pregnant should not drink before or during the pregnancy, nor while breast-feeding. If a woman is a heavy drinker or addicted to alcohol, she should avoid pregnancy until she is able to abstain from (completely quit) drinking.

The alcohol a pregnant woman drinks reaches the fetus within a few minutes. Alcohol passes through the placenta (the sac surrounding and nourishing the fetus) to the growing fetus. Because the baby is

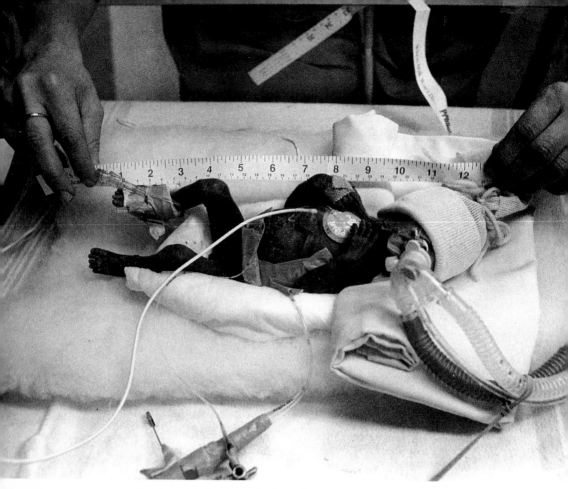

Babies with fetal alcohol syndrome are often born prematurely and may spend several weeks or even months in the hospital when they are born.

not yet mature, its system takes longer to break down the alcohol. The alcohol level in the fetus's blood is often higher than in the mother's, and it stays higher for a longer time. This exposure to alcohol can cause a lifetime of damage.

The amount of damage depends on the frequency, quantity, and timing of the mother's alcohol consumption. Every woman's body is unique and has its own response to alcohol. No one knows for sure how much alcohol it takes to hurt a fetus. We do know that several drinks in a short period of time are more harmful than the same amount spread out over a week. Drinking alcohol during different stages of pregnancy affects the fetus in different ways. However, the central nervous system and the brain grow throughout pregnancy and are affected at no matter what stage alcohol is consumed. The safest plan for a pregnant woman is to avoid alcoholic beverages completely. In addition, a pregnant woman should always check with her doctor before taking *any* medication.

Pregnant women who drink alcohol may have problems with their pregnancy. They may have a miscarriage, losing the baby long before it is ready to be born. They may have a stillborn baby, one that is born dead.

Some women who drink while pregnant have premature babies. These babies are born before they are completely developed. They can survive outside the mother's body with medical assistance. Premature babies usually stay in the hospital for a long time after they are born. They can be hard to care for and often have physical problems.

CHAPTER 3

The Signs and Symptoms of FAS

*B*abies with FAS are different from other babies. Doctors and nurses say that some babies smell like alcohol when they are born. Some are even born drunk. These infants are born addicted to alcohol. They often suffer withdrawal symptoms during their first few months.

Each infant with FAS is different. Some suffer more damage than others from their mother's drinking. But all babies with FAS have some things in common, including specific signs and types of behavior.

With a low birth weight and short length, a baby with FAS is small and thin when it is born. It has a small head, a flattened nose, a thin upper lip, and small eyes. It may have physical problems, including hearing defects or teeth growing in wrong, or defects of the heart, kidneys, muscles, joints, or sexual organs. Sometimes babies with FAS need surgery.

All babies born with FAS are also born with permanent damage to their brain and central nervous system. They often have learning problems that appear as the child grows. These are discussed later in the chapter. Sometimes it is difficult to tell if a baby has FAS. Some babies are born with FAE, meaning that they suffer from their mother's prenatal drinking but do not have all the symptoms present in an infant with FAS.

A Baby with FAS

It is difficult to be the parent of a baby with FAS. Some are called "failure to thrive" babies; they lose weight after they are born. They have poor sucking reflexes, which means that they do not reach for food the way most babies do. Sometimes babies with FAS have no desire to eat. One mother said it took her adopted baby with FAS three hours to finish a four-ounce bottle of milk.

Babies with FAS also have trouble

Children with FAS develop and learn at a much slower rate than children without FAS.

sleeping. They do not develop a regular sleeping schedule. They tend to be irritable and fussy. Some do not like to be held. They wiggle and squirm. It is difficult to comfort or quiet a baby with FAS.

Babies with FAS are slow to talk. It takes them longer to learn how to put words together. Learning language is a lifelong problem for people born with FAS or FAE. They are also slow to learn to walk and to be toilet-trained. Some still need diapers at five years of age.

Many babies born with FAS are placed

in foster care or given up for adoption. One study found that only one third of children with FAS were living with their biological parent. Another study found that half the mothers of children with FAS were dead. The women who are at the greatest risk of having babies with FAS are single, poor, uneducated, and older.

Kerry

Kerry's mom was an alcoholic. Her drink of choice was vodka, which she drank all day. Kerry's dad pretended not to notice. He stayed away from home as much as possible by working long hours. Kerry and her mom fought a lot. Kerry couldn't stand living at home. She felt lucky that she had Randy.

Randy and Kerry had been going out for two years. They planned to get married after graduation. Kerry's mom said she was too young to be thinking about marriage, but Kerry knew what she wanted. She knew that Randy really loved her.

Randy and Kerry spent all their time together. No matter how bad things were at home, she always looked forward to being with him. Then Kerry discovered that she was pregnant. She told her mother, then she said that she was going to marry Randy. Kerry's mom was furious. She screamed that

24 | *Kerry was no good, that she would have Randy arrested for rape. She said that Kerry could never see Randy again. Kerry was terrified. She knew how violent her mother got when she drank. She was afraid for Randy's safety.*

Kerry promised not to see Randy again. She dropped out of school to have the baby.

Kerry sat home all day and watched television. She was scared and depressed. She missed Randy. She even missed going to school. The only people she ever saw were her mother and father. Her father hardly ever spoke to her, and her mother spoke to her only when she had been drinking. Then she would scream and call her terrible names.

Kerry was scared, lonely, and angry. She wanted to get back at her mother, so one day she tried her mother's vodka. It tasted awful. She tried mixing it with orange juice, which made it taste better. When Kerry drank she could ignore her mother. Sometimes she even shouted back. Kerry drank all through the rest of her pregnancy.

Kerry's baby was born with FAS. *The baby was small and funny-looking, and she cried and fussed a lot. Kerry, however, was determined to provide the best for her baby girl. She felt so guilty for harming her baby.*

As a pregnant woman, every decision you make about drinking affects both you, your baby and your baby's future.

Kerry joined Alcoholics Anonymous. She learned how to get sober and stay sober. She started seeing Randy again. He wanted to marry her and help with the baby. Together they worked to give the baby everything they could. But no matter how much they loved her and how hard they tried, their baby would never be normal. She would never learn like other children. She would always need extra care.

What Is a Child with FAS Like?

It is difficult to be a child with FAS. The average IQ of a person with FAS is 65,

26 as opposed to the "normal" IQ of 100. Young children with FAS are shorter and weigh less than other children the same age. They have problems talking and learning language. They also have other learning disabilities, including the following:

- Difficulty generalizing information
- Difficulty matching words and behavior
- Difficulty mastering new skills or remembering something they have recently learned, such as tying shoelaces
- Spotty memory; remembering something that happened a year ago but not the day before
- Inflexibility of thought; they can only understand one concept expressed in one way. Once it is learned in that way, they don't easily understand it in another context.
- Difficulty predicting outcomes. A child with FAS may not be able to tell what will happen when he knocks over a glass of milk; he also tends to make the same mistakes over and over again.
- Difficulty distinguishing fact from fantasy; a person with FAS watching a

Someone born with FAS needs a lot of extra care and attention for the rest of her life.

television show thinks it is happening in real life.

• Difficulty distinguishing friends from strangers; he may meet someone once for five minutes and consider him a friend.

Children with FAS tend to be friendly and outgoing, which can actually cause problems for them. They like to touch and kiss a lot. They want to be held more than other children. It is natural for children to be afraid of people they do not know; it protects them from those who might hurt them. Children with FAS don't have this natural caution. They are friendly with everyone, even someone new. This puts them in greater danger of being sexually molested than most children. Parents of children with FAS need to watch them carefully.

Children with FAS are impulsive. They do things without thinking. For instance, they may run out in the street. They may wander away from their parents in a crowd. They may go off with a stranger. Children with FAS often do not learn from experience. They tend to have poor judgment. They do not always understand the consequences of their actions.

Children with FAS are extremely trusting and affectionate.
This could lead them into danger because they do not
understand that there are people who could hurt them.

30

These children are usually hyperactive—they cannot sit still. They are into everything. They have trouble understanding rules and following directions because they cannot hold still long enough to listen to them. When they do listen they have difficulty understanding the words.

A student who has these problems has trouble in school. He cannot sit still and listen. He cannot understand or follow directions. He often bothers other students by trying to touch or hug them. He wants all the teacher's attention. A child with FAS may be placed in special education classes where he can get extra attention. He will probably need extra help and be a slow learner throughout his schooling and for the rest of his life.

These difficulties mean that, for a child with FAS, it is harder to do well in school and harder to fit in. All these problems are a result of his mother's drinking.

Tami

Tami was ready to scream. She hated math class. She just didn't get it. No matter how hard she tried, she didn't understand. The teacher, Mr. Ceder, was really nice. He met

A teen with FAS may find schoolwork, particularly math, very difficult.

with her at lunch and after school sometimes. But she was still failing the class.

Tami was born with FAS. Her mother drank throughout her pregnancy. In fact, she was drunk when Tami was born. Tami was born prematurely, and she was very small. She stayed in the hospital for several weeks after she was born.

When Tami was six months old, she was released from the hospital. She went to live as a foster child with her aunt and uncle. The courts had said her mother was not fit to care for Tami. Tami's father did not want to take care of her. He was an alcoholic too.

Child Protective Services decided that her aunt and uncle would be good parents for her.

Everybody in school liked Tami. Ever since she could remember, people had called her China Doll—maybe because of her black hair and black eyes, or maybe because she was always the smallest person in her class. In grade school some of the other children even carried her around like a doll.

Still, school was really hard for Tami. Adding and subtracting seemed impossible. She was held back a couple of grades. Then, after some tests, she was placed in a special class for part of the day. The other students in the class had learning problems, too. After that, school was better for Tami. The class was structured so that the teacher had enough time to spend with each pupil who needed it. Tami finally felt that she could understand at least some of her math problems.

What Is a Teen with FAS Like?

According to the booklet "Fetal Alcohol Syndrome/Fetal Alcohol Effects" by Diane Malbin, one middle school student drew a picture of himself in a jail cell, with one arm reaching through the bars. In his hand he held a broomstick that was

Adolescence is a difficult period for everyone, but it is especially difficult for someone with FAS. This is often when teens with FAS begins to notice the physical and developmental differences between themselves and their peers.

34 stretched toward the key to his cell, which was hanging on a nearby wall. The boy said, "And the broomstick is just an inch too short. Happens all the time."

Being a teenager is difficult for everyone. For teens with FAS it is extra hard. In general, the problems they face in grade school just seem to get worse in middle and high school. Teens with FAS fall farther behind their peers. Arithmetic is an especially hard subject for them. They have trouble finishing assignments, paying attention in class, or learning new skills. During this time teenagers with FAS begin to notice how they are different from their peers. The differences in learning are greater with every year. FAS teens are likely to be smaller than others in their class. It is even hard to keep up in sports and physical education class.

Other students often tease teenagers with FAS or try to get them to do reckless or dangerous things such as stealing or calling a teacher a name. They are easily manipulated by others. They have poor judgment and do not always understand the consequences of their actions. A teen with FAS may lie and steal because he doesn't understand that it is wrong. He may try something dangerous on a dare.

Because of all these problems, an FAS
teenager may not feel good about himself.
He may have low self-esteem. He may get
depressed or even suicidal. He may start
drinking or using illegal drugs in an at-
tempt to feel better. He or she may become sexually active to get love and
attention.

A teenager with FAS may know he is different but not know the reason. He may
not have been diagnosed as having FAS.
His parents and teachers may not know.
It may be a relief for him to discover that
he has a specific disorder. He may feel that
at least there is a name for what is wrong
with him and a reason for his problems.

It is often a relief for parents and
teachers to discover what is wrong, too.
They can help a teenager with FAS better
if they understand what is wrong. They
can concentrate on helping him learn life
skills and vocational skills. He can learn
how to handle daily responsibilities and
chores. He can also learn how to keep a
job. A teen with FAS needs structure in his
life to help keep him safe and away from
trouble.

David

David was in the principal's office again. It

People with FAS function very well in a structured environment, such as a job with very specific tasks like setting the table.

seemed he was always in trouble. He had been in special education classes since third grade. He hated those classes. Sometimes he just lost his temper. Other times his classmates made fun of him or dared him to do things. This time Cory had told him to put glue in the VCR. The teacher was furious.

His teacher, the counselor, and the principal all said, "Can't you think before you do something? If your friends told you to jump off a cliff, would you?" Sometimes he thought he would. Sometimes he thought about killing himself. He was tired of having everybody mad at him all the time. David, *his two younger brothers, and one of his younger sisters were all diagnosed with FAS.*

David had a difficult home life. Both of his parents drank and fought a lot. The police often arrested his father, but he always came back and started drinking again. His mother never stopped. Sometimes his parents went out to bars and didn't come home for a couple of days. The kids were often left with little or no food in the house. Sometimes there was no heat either. Being the oldest, David tried to take care of his younger brothers and sisters by stealing food or taking them to their aunt's house during those times.

Sometimes David's teacher asked the school social worker to check on David's situation at home. One teacher really liked David and tried to help him. David even went to live with this teacher for a while. But he got homesick, and he was worried about his brothers and sisters.

David had one friend named Jameel. Jameel's mom drank a lot, too. Sometimes when she passed out, Jameel and David drank her beer. One time they took the car keys and drove around. The police stopped them and took them to jail because they had been drinking and driving.

David had to go to court for drinking and driving and for driving without a license.

Teens with FAS often feel depressed or even suicidal.

The judge ruled that David should get help for his drinking at an alcohol treatment center.

David liked the center. They had a schedule that everyone had to stick to. David liked having every day planned. It was easier for him not to have so many choices. He was able to meet with counselors and other people like him in group meetings. David got to talk about his problems and his feelings. His ideas even helped others at the center. He discovered that there were other people with problems like his. He learned that it was his mother's drinking that had given him fetal alcohol syndrome, the cause of most of his problems. He became angry with his mother. Talking about it helped.

David worried about his younger brothers and sister. He missed his mom and dad, too, even though he was mad at them for drinking. He still loved them.

Although David will always need the support and structure he receives at the clinic, he is learning the skills he needs to succeed in life.

What Is an Adult with FAS Like?

Most people with FAS have trouble learning about math, numbers, and money. They have a hard time sticking to a

40 budget, handling money, or making change. They also live for the moment. They have difficulty with the concept of time, so scheduling and planning time can be challenging. Because of this and other symptoms, it can be difficult for a person with FAS to live on his own.

Adults have described themselves in "Fetal Alcohol Syndrome/Fetal Alcohol Effects":

- A woman felt as though she had to "memorize life" in order to succeed. She has succeeded as a professional and an administrator.
- A man described himself as "the man with a mind like a steel sieve."
- Another man said his brain was like "Swiss cheese."

Adults, like children, with FAS thrive in a structured environment where they have the time they need to understand what's going on around them. Because they tend to be easily distracted, have spotty memories, and have trouble distinguishing fantasy from reality, among other things, they may have trouble functioning in many environments. Some people with FAS live in group homes with others like

Some people with FAS continue to need supervision into their adult lives.

42 | themselves. Others stay with their families. Some need supervision even as adults. Some end up homeless on the streets. Because of the trouble people with FAS can get into, such as stealing, there are also many adults with FAS in prisons.

It is possible for adults with FAS or FAE to live happy, successful lives. It requires patience, hard work, and understanding both by the victim and his family, but it is possible.

Whether you are battling an addiction to alcohol or just want more information on the effects of alcohol on your body and your baby, talk to a counselor.

CHAPTER 4

Learning Who Is at Risk

*W*e all pay the price for babies born with FAS or FAE. FAS costs our country millions of dollars. The National Institute of Alcohol Abuse and Alcoholism estimated in 1993 that it costs $1.5 million per person to deal with problems related to FAS over a lifetime. We pay for sheltered homes, special education programs, and social and health care workers to help FAS and FAE individuals and their families.

The cost to the person with FAS and his family is high, too. Every day the family has to deal with problems like poor health, learning difficulty, and bad behavior. Every day the family and the person with FAS live knowing that these problems didn't have to happen.

FAS and FAE are preventable. No child has to be born with these birth defects. Who is at risk for having a baby with FAS? How can these women be identified and helped when they are pregnant or even before they are pregnant? One test that social workers and medical professionals have found useful is called the TWEAK test. On a separate sheet of paper, answer these questions for yourself.

TWEAK Test

T	Tolerance: How may drinks can you hold?
W	Have your friends or relatives worried or complained about your drinking in the past year?
E	Eye-Opener: Do you sometimes take a drink in the morning when you first wake up?
A	Amnesia: Has a friend or family member ever told you about things you said or did while you were drinking that you could not remember?
K(C)	Do you sometimes feel the need to Cut Down on your drinking?

A 7-point scale is used to score this test. The tolerance question scores two

Fathers-to-be can be a great help to pregnant women by supporting their decision not to drink.

points if a woman reports that she can hold more than five drinks without falling asleep or passing out. A positive response to the worry question scores two points, and a positive response to the last three questions scores one point each. A score of two or more points indicates that the woman is likely to be an at-risk drinker.

Are you at risk for having a baby with FAS? Women who score as at-risk drinkers can get help. They need to understand that drinking can hurt their unborn babies. Health and social workers can work with them to reduce or eliminate their drinking. These women can join support groups such as Alcoholics Anonymous. They can go into alcohol detoxification programs. There are local and national sources of support. These groups teach strategies to help them recover from their addiction to alcohol. A support group can help a woman make the decision to stay sober and have a healthy baby.

Cheryl

Cheryl was a good student and had plans to go to college. She also liked to party on weekends. She figured she deserved to party since she worked so hard during the week. Cheryl and her boyfriend, Rodney, together

48   *with a bunch of friends drove out to some deserted spot and drank every weekend. Everyone tried to see who could drink the most. People would often drink until they threw up or passed out. Everyone in their group did it.*

One day Cheryl noticed that her period was late. Her period was very regular so she was pretty sure that she was pregnant. Cheryl went to the drugstore and bought a pregnancy testing kit. Her test was positive.

Next Cheryl went to a health clinic. The nurse had her do another pregnancy test. The doctor examined her and asked her about her last period. She told Cheryl that she was about a month pregnant. The doctor asked Cheryl many questions about her health and her habits.

One set of questions the doctor asked was the TWEAK test, the test designed to show whether Cheryl might be an at-risk drinker. Cheryl told the doctor that she could drink five beers without passing out. She also told the doctor that she sometimes didn't remember what she said or did when she was drinking. This gave Cheryl a score of 3 points, which identified her as an at-risk drinker.

Then the nurse explained to Cheryl that her drinking could hurt her unborn baby. She showed Cheryl pictures of babies born with FAS. *She told Cheryl about the birth defects called* FAS *and* FAE. *She told her that even if she had been drinking up until now, it was important to quit. Quitting drinking at any time during pregnancy increases the chances of having a healthy baby.*

The nurse told Cheryl about a support group sponsored by the health clinic. Pregnant women met once a week to discuss their experiences. A nurse met with them to answer questions. The women in the group supported each other. They committed themselves to eat right and exercise. They learned ways of avoiding alcohol. Cheryl decided to join the group. She found that she enjoyed talking to other women who were pregnant, sharing their experiences, and learning new ways to enjoy life without alcohol.

Cheryl and Rodney decided to get married. Six months later Cheryl gave birth to a healthy baby girl, Jessica. The young couple were proud that they had a healthy baby.

A pregnant teen who is concerned with her baby's health and safety will say no to alcohol no matter who offers it.

CHAPTER 5

How to Prevent FAS and FAE

*T*here are many unresolved issues and problems related to FAS and FAE. There are no easy answers to the following questions:

- Should pregnant alcoholics be physically restrained to keep them from drinking?
- Should adults with FAS be allowed to have children? Will they be able to care for them properly?
- Should pregnant women who drink be charged with child abuse?
- What should you do if a pregnant friend or relative drinks?
- Should doctors be responsible for telling women not to drink?

52

- Should women who have one or more children with FAS be allowed to have more children?
- Should companies that produce or sell alcohol be liable for victims of FAS?

A waiter in Oregon was so concerned about the damage alcohol might cause that he refused to serve a drink to a pregnant woman. The woman was very angry and complained to the manager. The waiter lost his job. After what you have learned in this book, what do you think you would have done if you had been the waiter?

One father sued the company that produced the alcohol that damaged his child. He lost the case, but others may try to do the same thing.

A judge on a Native American reservation said he would lock up pregnant women who were drinking. Other judges have said they charge pregnant women who drink with child abuse. Another said he has threatened pregnant women with jail time to get them to go to treatment programs for alcoholism.

Prevention

There is some good news. Studies show

that more and more women are aware
that drinking alcohol during pregnancy
can cause birth defects. Education is es-
sential in preventing FAS.

53

Some pregnant women, however, cannot simply stop drinking even though
they know how dangerous it is to their
unborn babies. These women are alcoholics. They are addicted to alcohol.
Alcoholics need help to stop drinking
and to learn how to deal with life while
sober. The cost of helping these women
is far less than the $1.5 million it costs
to care for a child with FAS over his lifetime. Programs that offer alcoholics support are listed in the back of this book.

FAS has been studied for over 20 years.
We now know many more ways of work-
ing with FAS and FAE children and adults.
When Michael Dorris adopted his son,
Adam, no one knew what was wrong with
Adam. Today teachers and counselors
and parents are much better informed.
They have learned how individuals with
FAS learn and how best to teach them.

What You Can Do

You can help prevent FAS. First, if you are
a woman and plan to become pregnant,
quit drinking at least three months ahead

Fathers play a vital role in their children's lives by encouraging their mother to be healthy while she is pregnant and by setting a good example for them after they are born.

of time. If you find out you are pregnant, stop drinking. If you find you cannot stop drinking, get help. The sooner you quit, the better it will be for your baby.

If you are a man, remember that fathers play an important role. The saying "A pregnant woman never drinks alone" has two meanings. The first is that her unborn baby "drinks" the alcohol too. The second is that the woman often drinks with someone, often the father. It is important that the father support the pregnant woman by not drinking himself, or at least by not drinking around her.

Friends can support a mother-to-be by having healthful, nonalcoholic drinks at parties and social gatherings rather than serving alcohol.

Because of the high rates of alcoholism in Native American communities, several of these communities have started FAS prevention programs. These programs provide education and support groups. Interesting activities focusing on things other than drinking are provided for young people. Elders are involved in helping and teaching young people to make healthy choices. Traditional healing practices are used as well as modern detoxification programs.

You can support your friend's choice not to drink alcohol by not serving any at your next party.

Each individual and community can work to find their own answers to FAS prevention. Through support groups and newsletters, groups, individuals, and communities can share what they have learned. It has only been 20 years since FAS was first identified. Because of the hard work and caring of many people, we know a lot more today. Together we can all use this knowledge to some day wipe out the number-one cause of mental retardation in the West.

Glossary
Explaining New Words

addiction Compulsive physical or psychological need for a habit-forming substance.

alcohol abuse Consumption of alcohol to the extent that problems result from use.

Alcoholics Anonymous A fellowship of men and women who share their experiences and problems with alcohol to help themselves and others recover from alcoholism.

fetal alcohol effects (FAE) The presence of one or more birth defects caused by alcohol use during pregnancy.

fetal alcohol syndrome (FAS) A group of physical and mental birth defects resulting from a woman's drinking during pregnancy.

fetus Unborn baby.

premature Born too soon.

prenatal The time before birth.

teratogen Any substance that causes abnormalities in the fetus.

58 | **withdrawal symptoms** Physical problems and discomfort, like shaking, headaches, and nausea, caused by no longer using a drug.

Help List

National Organization on Fetal Alcohol Syndrome
181 H Street, NW
Washington, DC 20006
800 66-NOFAS

National Institute on Alcohol Abuse and Alcoholism
PO Box 2345
Rockville, MD 20852
800 729-6686

NAPARE (National Association for Perinatal Addiction Research and Education)
11 East Hubbard Street
Chicago, IL 60611
800 638-2229 (Toll free help line)

Al-Anon/Alateen Family Group Headquarters
PO Box 862, Midtown Station
New York, NY 10018
212 351-9500

60 **Alcohol and Drug Dependency Information and Counseling Services (ADDICS)**
#2, 2471 1/2 Portage Avenue
Winnipeg, MB R3J 0N6
Canada

Alcoholics Anonymous, Toronto
#502 Intergroup Office
234 Eglinton Avenue E
Toronto, ON M4P 1K5
Canada

Also use your telephone book to find the local chapters of Al-Anon and Alateen. If you are pregnant, contact your doctor or local health or prenatal clinic.

For Further Reading

Dorris, Michael. *The Broken Cord*. New York: HarperCollins, 1990.

Englemann, Jeanne. *A Woman's Loss of Choice, A Child's Future*. Center City, MN: Hazeldon Educational Resources, 1993.

Graeber, Laurel. *Are You Dying for a Drink? Teenagers and Alcohol Abuse*. New York: Julian Messner, 1985.

Learn About Alcohol and Pregnancy. Center City, MN: Hazeldon Educational Materials, 1993.

Learn About Fetal Alcohol Syndrome and Fetal Drug Effects. Center City, MN: Hazeldon Educational Materials, 1993.

Miner, Jane Claypool. *Alcohol and You*. New York: Franklin Watts, 1988.

Nielson, Nancy J. *Teen Alcoholism*. San Diego: Lucent, 1990.

Nielson, Nancy, and Hurwitz, Sue. *Drugs and Birth Defects*. New York: The Rosen Publishing Group, 1993.

62 | *Videos*

New York State Disabilities Council.
 Mary's Choice. Albany: Productions
 KIKO, 1994.
Teens and Alcohol: The Hidden Problem.
 Pleasantville, NY: Sunburst Commu-
 nications: 1989.
Alateen Tells It Like It Is. New York:
 Al-Anon Family Groups, 1987.

Newsletters

Iceberg
FAS Information Service
PO Box 4292
Seattle, WA 98104

FAS and Other Drugs Update
Prevention Resource Center
822 South College Street
Springfield, IL 62704

FANN (Fetal Alcohol Network Newsletter)
158 Rosemont Avenue
Coatsville, PA 19320

Index

About the Author

Amy Nevitt received her B.A. from the University of New Mexico and her M.A. in counseling from Western New Mexico University. She has worked with teenagers for over 18 years, first as an English teacher, and for the last nine years as a librarian/media specialist.

Ms. Nevitt spent three years working on a Navajo reservation in New Mexico, and currently lives and works on the Zuni reservation there.

Photo Credits

Cover, p. 12 by Michael Brandt; pp. 2, 18 © Ansell Horn/ Impact Visuals; pp. 8, 29, 41 by Kim Sonsky/Matt Baumann; pp. 13, 25, 31, 38, 41 by Kim Sonsky; p. 22 © M. Brodskaya/ Impact Visuals; p. 27 © Evan Johnson/Impact Visuals; p. 44 by Katherine Hsu; all other photos by Kathleen McClancy.